Explorations of the Soul

Alexa Murphy

Index

Alexa Murphy

The Inner Journey

The inner journey is a journey that we are all destined to undertake at some point in our lives. This journey is not to a physical place, but to the deepest part of our being, to that hidden corner where our purest essence resides, our soul. Often, in the daily routine, we find ourselves so absorbed in responsibilities, in work, in relationships and in external concerns, that we forget to stop and look inward. However, it is in that pause, in that moment of introspection, where the true inner journey begins.

The inner journey is, in many ways, a process of discovery. It's like entering a vast unknown forest, where every step we take leads us to discover something new about ourselves. At first, it may seem overwhelming, even scary. We face our own shadows, fears and doubts that we have buried for years. But it is precisely in the courage to confront these aspects of ourselves where the opportunity for growth and transformation lies.

This journey does not follow a straight path nor does it have a fixed destination. There are no maps or guides to tell us exactly where to go. Each of us must chart our own path, learning to trust our intuition, that inner voice that, although sometimes faint, always guides us in the right direction. As we continue on this journey, we begin to strip away layers and layers of conditioning, limiting beliefs, and expectations that have been imposed on us, or that we have assumed without question. It is a process of liberation, where we begin to leave behind what does not serve us, what does not resonate with our deepest truth.

Throughout the inner journey, it is common to encounter moments of loneliness. This loneliness, however, should not be seen as something negative. It is in those moments of solitude where we truly meet our soul, where we can hear more clearly what we truly long for, what gives us peace and fills us with joy. It is a time to reconnect with ourselves, to recharge our energies and to reflect on what we have learned along the way.

The inner journey also invites us to explore our spirituality, to ask ourselves about the meaning of life, about our connection with the universe, with something bigger than ourselves. These questions, although profound, are essential to our growth. It is not about finding definitive answers, but about being open to possibilities, allowing ourselves to question and explore without fear. As we explore these dimensions, we begin to feel a deeper connection with our own soul and with the world around us.

Throughout this journey, it is crucial to practice patience and compassion towards ourselves. There will be days when we will feel lost, when we will doubt our progress, but it is important to remember that the inner journey is not rushed. Every step we take, no matter how small, brings us closer to our true self. And every setback, every obstacle we encounter along the way, is an opportunity to learn and grow.

This journey is also an act of self-love. By taking the time to know ourselves better, to care for ourselves, and to nourish our souls, we are cultivating a deep and lasting love for ourselves. This love is not selfish; It is the foundation on which we can build healthier relationships, live fuller lives, and contribute more meaningfully to the world around us.

Ultimately, the inner journey is a journey toward authenticity. It is a process of remembering who we really are, beyond the masks we have worn, beyond the expectations others have placed on us. It is a return to our essence, to that place within us that has always been there, waiting to be rediscovered. And although the journey never ends, each step we take brings us closer to living a life in harmony with our soul, a life full of purpose, peace and joy.

This journey, although challenging, is deeply rewarding. It allows us to see the world with new eyes, from a broader and more compassionate perspective. It teaches us to value what really matters, to let go of what does not serve us and to live more consciously and fully. So, if you are ready to embark on this inner journey, remember that you are not alone. Every step you take is an act of courage and love, and every discovery you make is a gift that will bring you closer to the true peace and satisfaction that can only be found by connecting with your soul.

Understanding the Soul

Understanding the soul is a topic that has fascinated humanity since time immemorial. Throughout history, different cultures and religions have tried to explain what the soul is and what its purpose is in our lives. Although the definition of soul can vary depending on beliefs, there is a general consensus that the soul is that part of us that transcends the physical, connecting us to something beyond our earthly existence. It is what makes us who we are, what gives meaning and depth to our lives.

The soul is perceived as the purest essence of our existence, something that cannot be seen or touched, but that we feel in the depths of our being. It's that inner whisper that guides us, that feeling we get when something "just feels right" or "just doesn't feel right." It is in the soul where our true identity resides, beyond the labels that society places on us, beyond the roles we play in our daily lives. Understanding the soul is, in essence, understanding who we really are.

From a spiritual perspective, the soul is immortal. This means that, unlike the physical body which eventually perishes, the soul continues its journey beyond death. For many traditions, this implies that the soul carries with it the experiences, learning and wisdom acquired in each life. It is like a living library, where all our experiences, emotions and decisions are stored. For this reason, some people believe in reincarnation, the idea that the soul returns to life in a new body to continue its learning and evolution.

The soul is also related to our purpose in life. Many people feel, at some point in their lives, an inner calling, a voice that tells them that there is something else they need to do or be. This call is, in many cases, the voice of the soul that tries to guide us towards our true path. Ignoring this voice can lead to feelings of dissatisfaction, being out of alignment, or even emptiness. On the other hand, when we hear and follow this call, we feel more connected to ourselves and the world, experiencing a deep sense of peace and contentment.

Despite its intangible nature, the soul has a profound impact on our daily lives. It is the source of our deepest emotions, our passions and our desires. When we are in tune with our soul, our actions and decisions reflect our truest values, allowing us to live more authentically and fully. On the other hand, when we disconnect from our soul, we can feel lost, confused or even unmotivated, as if something is missing in our life.

Understanding the soul also involves recognizing its relationship with the mind and body. While the soul is our spiritual essence, the mind is the center of our thoughts and reasoning, and the body is the physical vehicle that allows us to experience the world. These three aspects of our being are interconnected and influence each other. For example, when the soul is at peace, the mind tends to be calmer, and the body healthier. On the contrary, when we ignore the needs of the soul, we can experience anxiety, stress, or even physical illness. This shows the importance of taking care of not only our body and mind, but also our soul.

For many people, understanding the soul is a lifelong process. It is not something that can be solved at once, but rather a path of continuous exploration. As we grow and face different challenges and experiences, our understanding of the soul also evolves. What we believe or understand about the soul at a young age can change as we gain more wisdom and perspective.

An important aspect of understanding the soul is acceptance. Accept that the soul has its own rhythm and its own way of evolving. We cannot always force or control this process. Sometimes the soul needs time to heal, to reflect or to adapt to new circumstances. Other times, it can surprise us with clarity or insight that we didn't expect. The key is to be patient and compassionate with ourselves as we navigate this process.

The soul connection can also be strengthened through spiritual practices. Meditation, for example, is a powerful tool for quieting the mind and listening to the voice of the soul. Through meditation, we can connect with our deepest essence, letting go of external distractions and turning our attention inward. Another practice is introspection, taking time to reflect on our experiences, emotions and desires, and how these reflect the needs of our soul.

In short, understanding the soul is a deeply personal journey that leads us to know our true essence. It is learning to listen to that inner voice that guides us and to recognize that there is something beyond the physical that defines us. It is a continuous process of growth and evolution, which requires patience, compassion and, above all, self-love. By embarking on this journey of understanding, we not only come closer to ourselves, but we also find greater peace and contentment in our lives. This is the gift that the soul offers us: the opportunity to live more authentically and fully, in harmony with our true nature.

Spiritual Awakening

Spiritual awakening is a profound and transformative process that can change the way we see the world and ourselves. It is as if a veil is suddenly lifted from our eyes, and we begin to see life with a new, deeper clarity. This awakening does not happen overnight; It is a gradual process that can be triggered by a variety of experiences, such as a personal crisis, the loss of a loved one, an illness, or even a simple moment of reflection that causes us to question our deepest beliefs and values.

When a person experiences a spiritual awakening, it is common for them to begin to feel disconnected from everyday life as they knew it before. Activities and concerns that previously occupied much of his time and energy may seem superficial or meaningless. He may feel a growing need to find something deeper, something that gives him more authentic and lasting meaning. This is a clear sign that the soul is looking for something beyond the material, something that allows it to connect with its true essence.

A central aspect of spiritual awakening is the feeling of connection to something larger than ourselves. It can be a connection with nature, with the universe, or with a higher force that we feel guides and supports us. This connection makes us feel that we are not alone, that we are part of a larger whole and that our lives have a deeper purpose. This feeling of connection is comforting and can bring an inner peace we have never experienced before.

During spiritual awakening, it is common for people to experience a reevaluation of their values and beliefs. What once seemed important may lose its relevance, and things that were previously ignored may take on new importance. For example, a person may begin to value deep, authentic relationships more, rather than superficial ones; or you may find a new interest in spirituality, meditation, or service to others. This reassessment is not always easy, as it may involve letting go of aspects of life that no longer serve us, but it is an essential part of the awakening process.

Spiritual awakening can also bring with it a greater sense of compassion and empathy toward others. By connecting more deeply with our own essence, we begin to see others in a different way, recognizing that we are all on a similar journey. This new perspective allows us to be more understanding and less judgmental, and prompts us to act with more love and kindness toward others. In some ways, spiritual awakening opens our hearts and allows us to see the world from a more loving and unified perspective.

It is important to note that spiritual awakening is not always a comfortable process. It can bring with it moments of confusion, uncertainty and even loneliness. As our old beliefs and ways of life crumble, we may feel lost or disoriented, not knowing exactly where we are headed. However, it is in these times of uncertainty where the opportunity for growth lies. By allowing ourselves to let go of the old, we create space for the new and authentic to enter our lives.

Throughout spiritual awakening, it is essential to learn to trust the process, even if we do not always understand what is happening. Trust that the soul knows what it needs and that each experience, no matter how difficult, has a purpose in our growth. This trust allows us to navigate awakening more easily and helps us stay calm in the midst of chaos.

During this process, many people discover the importance of introspection and reflection. Taking time to be silent, to meditate, or simply to be alone with our thoughts can be incredibly helpful. These moments of stillness allow us to connect more deeply with our soul, hear its voice, and gain clarity about the path we should follow. Introspection also helps us process the emotions and experiences that arise during awakening, allowing us to integrate them in a healthy way.

Spiritual awakening can also lead us to seek new forms of expression and creativity. As we connect more deeply with our essence, we may feel the urge to express what we are experiencing in new and creative ways. This can be through art, writing, music, or any other form of expression that allows us to share our inner experience with the world. This process of creation is not only therapeutic, but it can also be a way to inspire and connect with others.

Finally, it is important to remember that spiritual awakening is not a destination, but rather a continuous journey. There is no end point where we can say we have "arrived" or have "made it." Instead, it is a constant process of evolution and growth, where each new level of consciousness takes us to an even deeper one. This journey is unique to each person, and there is no "right" or "wrong" path to follow. The important thing is to be open and receptive to what the soul is showing us, and trust that, in the end, everything is happening for our highest good.

Spiritual awakening is a gift, an opportunity to reconnect with our true essence and live a more full, authentic and meaningful life. As we embark on this journey, we discover that life has a deeper purpose, and that purpose is aligned with our soul. We realize that everything we need for this journey is already within us, waiting to be discovered and embraced. It is a journey of transformation, love and discovery, which leads us to a deeper understanding of ourselves and the world around us.

The Connection with the Higher Being

The connection with the Higher Being is a fundamental aspect in the spiritual search and in the deep understanding of our existence. This concept, although it may seem abstract or difficult to grasp, actually refers to the idea that within each of us there is a higher, wiser part, which is in constant communication with the universe, with the divine, or with superior strength. This part of us, the Higher Self, is like an internal compass that guides us towards what is truly right and meaningful in our lives.

Throughout life, it is common for us to feel disconnected from this inner guidance. The daily pressures, responsibilities, external expectations, and distractions of the modern world can cloud our connection with the Higher Self. However, that connection is never completely lost; It is always there, waiting for us to turn our attention to it. Reconnecting with the Higher Self is an act of coming home, of remembering who we really are and what our purpose is in this life.

The connection with the Higher Being does not require complicated rituals or deep knowledge of spirituality. It is rather a process of quieting the mind, opening the heart and listening to that inner voice that has always been there. It is learning to trust our intuition, those feelings and hunches that guide us, and that we often ignore or overlook. The Higher Self communicates with us in subtle ways, through those small flashes of clarity, those moments when something just "clicks" and we know, without a doubt, what the correct path to follow is.

For many, the connection to the Higher Self is experienced most clearly through meditation. Meditation allows us to quiet the mind, reduce external and internal noise, and tune in to that higher frequency that is the Higher Being. By sitting in silence, focusing on the breath or a mantra, we can begin to feel a deep peace, a clarity that arises from the depths of our being. In those moments, we may receive insights, answers to questions we have been carrying in our hearts, or simply a feeling of well-being and connection that reminds us that we are on the right path.

Another important aspect of connecting with the Higher Self is trust. Trust that there is a part of us that always knows what is best, that is always connected to the divine, and that guides us toward our highest good. This trust is not always easy to cultivate, especially in a world where logic, reason, and control are so valued. However, trusting the Higher Self means letting go of control, stopping trying to force things and allowing life to unfold naturally, knowing that everything happens at the perfect time and in the perfect way.

The connection with the Higher Self also teaches us to live more authentically. As we strengthen this connection, we begin to align more with our inner truth, with what we truly want and need in our life. Decisions become clearer, paths open, and we find greater ease in life, because we are acting from a place of authenticity and not from fear, doubt, or external pressure. It is as if, by connecting with the Higher Being, our lives begin to flow more naturally and harmoniously.

A fascinating aspect of connecting with the Higher Self is that, although it is deeply personal, it also connects us to others and to the universe in a broader way. As we tune into our own inner wisdom, we also begin to see the wisdom in others, to recognize the divinity in all things. This connection allows us to live with more compassion, more empathy, and more love toward others. We understand that we are all on a similar journey, that we all have a Higher Being to guide us, and that our experiences, although unique, are interconnected.

Cultivating this connection is not a one-time thing; It is an ongoing process that requires practice and dedication. It is important to create moments in our daily lives where we can reconnect with the Higher Self, whether through meditation, prayer, reflection or simply taking time to be silent and peaceful. These moments allow us to recalibrate, return to our center and remember what really matters.

In addition to meditation, nature can be a powerful ally in connecting with the Higher Being. Spending time in nature, whether walking through a forest, sitting by the sea or simply observing the stars, allows us to reconnect with that part of us that is in tune with the universe. Nature reminds us of beauty, simplicity and the natural order of things, and helps us calm our minds and open our hearts.

It is also helpful to surround ourselves with people who support us on this path, who understand and value the importance of spiritual connection. Having a community, even a small one, that shares our beliefs and supports us in times of doubt or confusion can be of great help. These people can offer valuable perspectives, remind us of the importance of trusting the process, and share practices and experiences that enrich our own journey.

It is crucial to remember that connecting with the Higher Self is a unique process for each person. There is no right or wrong way to do it. For some, it can be a very spiritual and mystical experience, while for others it can simply be a feeling of peace and clarity. The important thing is to be open to what arises, without expectations or judgment, and allow the connection to develop naturally and authentically.

Ultimately, connecting with the Higher Self leads us to a life of greater fulfillment and purpose. It allows us to live in alignment with our truth, make decisions that reflect our deepest values, and find greater peace in the midst of life's challenges. It is a process of constant evolution and discovery, which invites us to explore the depths of our being and to live in a way that reflects our purest essence. By cultivating this connection, we not only improve our lives, but we also contribute to a more harmonious and connected world, where each of us plays an important role in the fabric of existence.

Alexa Murphy

The Power of Meditation

The power of meditation is something that many people have discovered over the centuries, and that more and more people are beginning to explore in today's world. Meditation is not just a technique to relax, but a powerful tool that can transform our lives in profound and lasting ways. Through meditation, we can learn to calm our mind, find peace in the midst of chaos, and connect with our deepest essence. It is a simple process in theory, but its effects can be extraordinary when practiced regularly.

Meditation can be understood as the act of focusing the mind on a single point, whether on the breath, on a mantra, on an image or simply on stillness. By doing so, we begin to reduce the mental noise that often dominates our consciousness. This noise includes incessant thoughts, worries, fears, and all the distractions that prevent us from being fully present in the moment. When we meditate, we train the mind to focus and become still, allowing the body and spirit to relax deeply.

One of the main benefits of meditation is stress reduction. In modern life, stress has become a constant for many people, affecting both physical and mental health. Meditation offers a refuge, a space where we can release tensions and allow our nervous system to relax. By spending time meditating, even if it's just a few minutes a day, we can experience a noticeable decrease in stress. This not only improves our overall health, but also makes us more resilient in the face of adversity.

In addition to reducing stress, meditation helps us gain mental clarity. When our mind is overloaded with thoughts and worries, it is difficult to make clear and wise decisions. Meditation acts as a mental cleanser, clearing clutter and allowing us to see things more clearly. This clarity helps us make decisions more aligned with our true desires and needs, and live a more authentic life. Instead of reacting impulsively to situations, we learn to respond in a more calm and considered manner.

Another powerful aspect of meditation is its ability to improve our relationship with ourselves. We are often our own worst critics, judging ourselves harshly for our imperfections and mistakes. Meditation teaches us to be kinder and more compassionate with ourselves. By sitting quietly and observing our thoughts without judging them, we learn to accept ourselves as we are. This acceptance does not mean complacency, but rather a loving understanding that we are constantly evolving beings, and that it is okay not to be perfect.

Meditation also strengthens our connection with others. By calming the mind and opening the heart, we become more aware of the emotions and needs of the people around us. We become more empathetic, more willing to listen to and understand others. This greater empathy improves our relationships, making them deeper and more meaningful. We become less reactive and more present in our interactions, which in turn promotes an environment of peace and harmony in our lives.

In addition to the emotional and mental benefits, meditation has positive physical effects. Numerous studies have shown that regular meditation can lower blood pressure, improve sleep quality, and strengthen the immune system. It can also help relieve chronic pain and improve your ability to concentrate. These physical benefits are a result of the stress reduction and promotion of deep relaxation that meditation facilitates. When the body relaxes, it enters a state of natural healing, allowing it to recover and regenerate more effectively.

A fascinating aspect of meditation is how it helps us connect with something bigger than ourselves. For many people, meditating is a way to tune into the universe, the divine, or a higher force. By quieting the mind, we create a space where we can feel that deeper, more spiritual connection. No matter what our beliefs, meditation can be a path to a greater understanding of our place in the world and our relationship with the sacred.

Meditation is a practice that can be customized to fit individual needs. There are many different ways to meditate, from moving meditation, such as yoga or tai chi, to guided meditation, where a voice guides us through the process. Some people prefer silent meditation, while others find it helpful to meditate to soft music or nature sounds. The important thing is to find an approach that resonates with us and that we can easily integrate into our daily lives.

For those who are new to meditation, it may seem difficult at first. The mind can be full of thoughts, and sitting in silence can be uncomfortable or frustrating. It is important to remember that meditation is not about emptying the mind completely, but rather about observing thoughts without clinging to them. Over time, as we continue to practice, the mind begins to calm naturally, and meditation becomes easier and more enjoyable. It is a gradual process that requires patience and perseverance, but the long-term benefits are immense.

Incorporating meditation into our daily routine can be as simple as spending a few minutes each morning or before bed. We don't need a lot of time or a special place; What matters is the intention to pause, to breathe deeply and to focus on the present moment. These moments of meditation, although brief, can have a significant impact on how we feel and how we face the day. Even on the busiest days, a couple of minutes of meditation can help us recharge and stay calm.

In short, meditation is a powerful practice that offers countless benefits for the body, mind, and spirit. It is a tool we can all use to improve our quality of life, reduce stress, increase mental clarity, and strengthen our connections with ourselves and others. Through meditation, we learn to live more consciously, to appreciate the present and to find peace in the midst of any circumstance. It is a simple, but deeply transformative practice that invites us to discover and experience the richness of our inner world.

The Importance of Inner Silence

Inner silence is a concept that, although it may seem simple, has a depth and importance that we often underestimate. We live in a world full of noise, both external and internal. We find external noise in daily life: traffic, conversations, news, notifications from our electronic devices. Internal noise, on the other hand, is that constant flow of thoughts, worries, and emotions that occupy our mind. This noise can be overwhelming and can make it difficult for us to connect with our true essence and what really matters.

Inner silence is the absence of this mental noise. It is that space in which, by quieting our mind, we can hear more clearly the voice of our deepest being. This silence is not simply the absence of sound, but a state of calm and mental stillness that allows us to be truly present and at peace. It is a state that can be achieved through practice and intention, and that has the power to transform our lives in significant ways.

One of the reasons why inner silence is so important is because it allows us to connect with our inner wisdom. In the hustle and bustle of everyday life, it's easy to lose sight of our true needs and desires. We let ourselves be carried away by external expectations, by what we think we should do or by what others expect of us. In this process, we can disconnect from what truly makes us happy and fulfilled. By cultivating inner silence, we create a space where we can reflect and tune in to what we really want and need. It is in this silence where we can listen to our intuition, that inner voice that knows what is best for us.

Inner silence is also essential for decision making. Often, when we are facing an important choice, our minds are filled with doubts, fears and contradictory thoughts. This mental noise can cloud our judgment and make it difficult for us to see clearly what the best path forward is. By entering a state of inner silence, we can clear this confusion and allow clarity to emerge. In silence, responses often appear naturally, without the need to force anything. This clarity allows us to make decisions that are more aligned with our values and our internal truth.

Another crucial aspect of inner silence is its ability to reduce stress and anxiety. Mental noise is one of the main sources of stress in our lives. When our mind is constantly busy, it is difficult to relax and enjoy the present moment. We worry about the future, ruminate about the past, and feel overwhelmed by the demands of the present. Inner silence, on the other hand, invites us to let go of these worries and find peace in the now. By practicing inner silence, we learn to not hold on to our thoughts and allow them to come and go without disturbing us. This practice helps us reduce mental and emotional tension, which in turn improves our overall well-being.

The practice of inner silence also strengthens our connection with the present. In modern life, it is easy to be physically present but mentally absent, caught up in our thoughts or worries. This prevents us from fully enjoying life's experiences and can affect our relationships with others. By cultivating inner silence, we learn to be more present in each moment, to appreciate what is happening here and now. This full presence allows us to experience life with greater intensity and meaning, and helps us create more vivid and satisfying memories.

Inner silence also opens the door to greater creativity. When our mind is free of noise and distractions, it creates space for ideas to flow more freely and naturally. Many artists, writers and creators find that their best ideas come in moments of silence and stillness. This state of mental calm allows inspiration to spring from the depths of our being, without being blocked by the noise of everyday thoughts. By practicing inner silence, we can access a wealth of creativity that we may not have known we had.

Furthermore, inner silence is a path to self-compassion and self-love. In the hustle and bustle of daily life, it's easy to fall into patterns of self-criticism and judgment. We push ourselves too hard, punish ourselves for our mistakes, and often forget to treat ourselves kindly. Inner silence offers us a space to reconnect with ourselves from a place of love and acceptance. In this state of stillness, we can listen to our own emotional needs and attend to them carefully. It is a time to nourish ourselves on a deep level, to remind ourselves that we deserve care and compassion, just as we are.

It is important to mention that cultivating inner silence is not always easy, especially at first. Our minds are used to being busy, and when we try to create silence, it is common for thoughts and emotions that we have been avoiding to arise. These moments may be uncomfortable, but they are an important part of the process. By allowing ourselves to feel and face what arises in the silence, we can begin to heal and release what no longer serves us. Over time, the practice of inner silence becomes more natural and pleasurable, and the benefits we experience become deeper and deeper.

Inner silence can also have a positive impact on our relationships. When we are at peace with ourselves, we are able to be more present and understanding of others. Mental noise often prevents us from truly listening to others, because we are too busy with our own thoughts. By practicing inner silence, we can learn to listen more carefully, be more open to the perspectives of others, and respond more thoughtfully. This improves the quality of our interactions and helps us build stronger, more meaningful relationships.

Finally, inner silence connects us with the sacred. Regardless of our spiritual beliefs, silence allows us to feel a deeper connection with the universe, with nature, or with the divine. It is in silence where we can experience a sense of unity and belonging to something bigger than ourselves. This sense of connection gives us peace and reminds us that we are not alone, that we are part of a vaster, more wonderful whole.

In short, inner silence is a powerful tool for personal transformation. It allows us to connect with our inner wisdom, reduce stress, improve our relationships, and live more present and authentic. Although it requires practice and patience, the benefits it brings are immense. By cultivating inner silence, we give ourselves the opportunity to live a fuller life, at peace with ourselves and in harmony with the world around us.

Self-Love as a Spiritual Basis

Self-love is a topic that, although it is often talked about in terms of self-esteem or confidence, has a much deeper dimension when we understand it as the basis of our spiritual life. Self-love, at its core, is the recognition and acceptance of our own worth. It is the understanding that we are complete and worthy beings, just as we are, and that we deserve care, respect and compassion. This self-love is not selfishness, but a fundamental need that allows us to live in peace with ourselves and the world around us.

When we talk about self-love as a spiritual foundation, we are referring to the idea that the spiritual journey begins from within. We cannot truly connect with the divine, the universe, or others fully and authentically if we have not first cultivated a deep love and respect for ourselves. This self-love is the root of our spirituality, the fertile soil in which our inner peace, our compassion, and our ability to love others grow.

Self-love leads us to acceptance of who we are at our deepest core. Throughout life, we can carry insecurities, doubts, and feelings of inadequacy that make us feel disconnected from our true essence. These burdens often come from external expectations, the judgments of others, or the mistakes and failures we have made. However, self-love invites us to let go of those burdens and see ourselves with eyes of compassion. It is recognizing that, although we are not perfect, we are worthy of love and respect. It is understanding that our mistakes do not define us, and that, like everyone, we are on a journey of growth and learning.

Self-love also teaches us to set healthy boundaries. When we really love and respect ourselves, we are able to say no to what harms us or distances us from our inner peace. This may mean distancing ourselves from toxic relationships, destructive habits, or situations that cause us unnecessary suffering. Setting limits is not an act of selfishness, but of self-care. It is protecting our physical, emotional and spiritual well-being, and creating a space where we can flourish and grow. By taking care of ourselves in this way, we are strengthening our spiritual foundation, allowing us to live more authentically and aligned with our truth.

Another important dimension of self-love as a spiritual foundation is the ability to forgive ourselves. Along the path of life, it is inevitable that we make mistakes, make decisions we later regret, or act in ways that do not reflect our deepest values. These moments can lead us to feel guilt or shame, emotions that distance us from our essence and that can obscure our connection with the spiritual. Self-love invites us to practice self-forgiveness, to let go of guilt, and to recognize that we are human, that we are learning, and that forgiveness is an essential part of the healing process.

Furthermore, self-love allows us to be more resilient in the face of life's challenges. When we love ourselves, we develop an internal foundation of strength that helps us face difficulties with more calm and confidence. We know that regardless of what is happening outside, we have an inner refuge where we can find comfort and support. This resilience allows us to stand firm in the midst of life's storms, and gives us the ability to recover and move forward with hope and determination.

Self-love is also the key to building healthy and meaningful relationships. When we value ourselves, we are able to establish relationships based on mutual respect and support. We do not look to others for validation that we lack, but rather we approach them from a place of plenitude and generosity. Self-love allows us to be authentic in our relationships, to show who we really are, without fear of judgment or rejection. This creates a solid foundation for genuine and deep connections, which enrich and nourish us on a spiritual level.

It is important to note that self-love is not a fixed or permanent state, but rather a continuous practice. It is something that we must cultivate every day, through our actions, thoughts and decisions. Sometimes, it can be difficult to maintain this self-love, especially in times of stress or difficulty, but it is precisely in those moments that it is most necessary. Practicing self-love means treating yourself with kindness, being patient with yourself, and remembering that we deserve care and attention, regardless of external circumstances.

A powerful way to cultivate self-love is through self-care practices that nourish us on a physical, emotional, and spiritual level. This can include activities such as meditation, exercise, journaling, or simply taking time to rest and relax. By dedicating time and energy to taking care of ourselves, we are sending a message to ourselves that we are important, that our well-being is a priority. These practices not only improve our health and well-being, but also strengthen our connection with ourselves and with the spiritual.

Self-love also helps us live more authentically. When we love and accept ourselves as we are, we feel freer to be who we really are, without the need to impress others or meet external expectations. This authenticity is essential for our spiritual growth, because it allows us to align with our inner truth and live in harmony with our values. By being authentic, we also inspire others to do the same, creating an environment of honesty and acceptance in our relationships and communities.

Finally, self-love connects us with universal love. When we cultivate love for ourselves, we realize that we are part of something bigger, a network of beings who also deserve love and respect. This recognition leads us to act with more compassion and empathy towards others, knowing that, by taking care of ourselves, we are also contributing to the well-being of others. Self-love, then, becomes a bridge to a broader and more universal love, which encompasses not only ourselves, but all living beings and the world as a whole.

In conclusion, self-love is the foundation on which our spiritual life is built. It is the foundation that allows us to connect with our essence, establish healthy relationships, face challenges with resilience and live authentically and fully. By cultivating self-love, we are nourishing our being at a deep level, creating fertile ground for our spiritual growth and for a life full of peace, joy and meaning. Although the path to self-love can be challenging, the fruits we reap in the process are immense and transformative, allowing us to live a richer life in harmony with the divine and ourselves.

The Healing of the Soul

Healing the soul is a deep and transformative process that leads us to a state of peace and inner well-being. This journey is not always easy, but it is one of the most important we can undertake in our lives. Throughout our experiences, our souls can accumulate wounds, caused by the pain, losses, disappointments and traumas we have faced. These wounds can manifest themselves in many ways: in feelings of sadness, in anxiety, in fears that prevent us from moving forward, or in a disconnection with our true essence. Healing the soul is the process of releasing these wounds, allowing ourselves to feel and process the pain, and finding peace and balance within ourselves.

Healing the soul begins with the recognition of our wounds. Often in our daily lives, we can be so busy or so focused on the outside that we ignore what is going on inside of us. It's easy to repress or deny pain, either out of fear of facing it or because we simply don't know how to handle it. However, this pain does not go away on its own. If we don't address it, it can grow and manifest in ways that negatively impact our lives. The first step toward healing the soul is to be willing to look within, to recognize the areas of our lives where we feel pain or discomfort, and to accept that these wounds exist.

Once we have recognized our wounds, the next step is to allow ourselves to feel them. This can be difficult, as it may involve reliving painful experiences or facing emotions that we have been avoiding. However, feeling the pain is a crucial part of the healing process. When we avoid our emotions, they stay trapped inside us, preventing us from moving forward. By allowing ourselves to feel the pain, we are releasing these emotions, giving them space to be processed and eventually released. This process may be uncomfortable, but it is a necessary step for healing.

Self-compassion is a key aspect in healing the soul. When we face our wounds, it is easy to fall into the trap of self-criticism or judgment. We may feel guilty about our emotions, or we may think that we should be stronger or more able to handle the pain. However, it is important to remember that we are all human, and that pain and hurt are a natural part of life. Self-compassion means treating yourself with the same kindness and care that you would offer a loved one who was going through a difficult time. It is recognizing that it is okay to feel pain, and that we deserve love and care as we heal.

Healing the soul also involves letting go of the past. Often our wounds are tied to events or people from the past that have caused us pain. Although we cannot change what has happened, we can choose how we respond to it. Letting go of the past does not mean forgetting or denying what happened, but rather stopping clinging to it in a way that causes us suffering. It is a process of liberation, of forgiveness, both towards others and towards ourselves. By letting go of the past, we are making space for the present, allowing our soul to free itself from the weight of what can no longer be changed, and focus on what we can do here and now for our well-being.

Another essential aspect of soul healing is the connection with our spiritual essence. As we heal, it is important to remember that we are not alone in this process. Whether we find comfort in nature, in meditation, in prayer, or in a connection with the divine, spiritual support can be a source of strength and guidance on our healing path. This connection reminds us that we are part of something bigger than ourselves, that there is a source of love and compassion always available to us. By nurturing our spiritual connection, we are nourishing our soul and strengthening our ability to heal.

Soul healing can also involve working with practices and techniques that help us release pain and restore balance to our being. This may include therapy, writing, visualization, conscious breathing, or any other practice that resonates with us. Each person is different, so it is important to find the tools that work best for us in our healing process. The important thing is to be persistent and patient, knowing that healing is a process that takes time and develops in layers. As we work on our healing, we may begin to feel gradual relief, a sense of peace and lightness that tells us we are moving on the right path.

The environment also plays an important role in the healing of the soul. Surrounding ourselves with people and situations that support us, that nourish us and that help us feel safe is essential. It is possible that in the healing process we need to distance ourselves from certain relationships or environments that cause us stress or that aggravate our wounds. This is not always easy, but it is an act of care for ourselves. By choosing an environment that supports us, we are creating a space where our soul can heal and flourish.

Additionally, it is important to remember that soul healing is not a destination, but rather a continuous journey. Throughout life, we will face new challenges and wounds that will require our attention and care. However, as we progress on our healing path, we become stronger and more able to handle pain and heal more effectively. Each healing experience teaches us something new about ourselves and brings us closer to our true essence.

Ultimately, soul healing brings us to a state of greater peace and wholeness. It allows us to let go of the weight of pain and wounds, and opens us to new possibilities of growth, love and connection. It is a process that, although challenging, is deeply rewarding, because it leads us to a more authentic life, more in tune with our true nature. By healing our soul, we are creating a space of inner peace that allows us to live with more joy, love and freedom.

In short, soul healing is an essential process for our well-being and spiritual growth. It requires courage, compassion, and a commitment to our own well-being. Through healing, we release the pain of the past, reconnect with our essence and create a space of peace and balance within us. Although the path may be difficult, the fruits of this journey are immense, leading us to a fuller, richer and more meaningful life. Soul healing is ultimately an act of love towards ourselves, a gift we give ourselves to live with more freedom, joy and connection with who we really are.

Intuition as a Spiritual Guide

Intuition is one of the most powerful and mysterious tools we have, and when we consider it as a spiritual guide, its value multiplies. Intuition is often described as that deep, almost inexplicable knowledge that arises within us, a feeling or a hunch that tells us what is right or what we should do in a given situation. Although we can't always explain why we feel a certain way or why a specific idea seems right, intuition has a way of guiding us that goes beyond logic and conventional reasoning.

Intuition can be seen as a direct connection with our soul, a path through which our deepest essence communicates with us. In a world full of noise and distractions, intuition acts as an internal compass, guiding us toward the path that most aligns with our truth and values. It is that soft, subtle voice that, when we listen to it, directs us toward decisions that resonate with our being, decisions that often lead us toward peace and balance.

Intuition often manifests itself in the form of a "gut feeling," a sensation in the stomach or heart that tells us something is right or wrong. It is possible that, at certain times, we feel attracted to an idea, a person or a place without knowing exactly why, but with the certainty that it is the right thing to do. This attraction is intuition working in us, guiding us toward experiences and people that are important to our spiritual growth and well-being.

Throughout history, many people have spoken of the power of intuition, from great thinkers and spiritual leaders to ordinary people who have trusted their intuition in critical moments. There are countless stories of people who have followed their intuition in difficult situations and found solutions that seemed impossible. This is because intuition, when cultivated and followed, has a way of guiding us toward outcomes that are aligned with our highest good, even when we can't see the big picture from our current perspective.

However, despite its power, intuition is often underestimated or overlooked. We live in a society that values rational thinking, logic and tangible evidence, which has its place and importance. But intuition operates on a different level. This is not just a hunch or a random idea; It is a form of knowing that comes from a deep place within us, a place that is in tune with what we need on a spiritual and emotional level. To truly harness the power of intuition, we need to learn to trust it, even when we don't have all the answers or when what it tells us goes against logic or external expectations.

Learning to listen to and trust our intuition can take time and practice. Sometimes intuition can be buried under layers of fear, doubt, or social conditioning. These obstacles can make it difficult to hear the voice of our intuition, but not impossible. The key to connecting with our intuition is inner silence and introspection. When we take the time to calm our minds and listen to what we really feel, we begin to tune into that inner voice that has always been there, waiting to be heard. This can be achieved through practices such as meditation, mindfulness, or simply spending time in nature, away from the noise and distractions of the world.

Additionally, it is important to remember that intuition does not always present itself in dramatic or obvious ways. Often, it is subtle, a slight tilt or a small nudge in a certain direction. We may not always feel a "big revelation moment" when we follow our intuition. Instead, we may notice a sense of peace or certainty, an inner tranquility that tells us we are on the right path. This tranquility is a sign that our intuition is guiding us well, and that we are aligned with our spiritual purpose.

As we learn to trust our intuition, we also become more aware of how it speaks to us. Some people experience intuition as a physical feeling, like a sensation in the chest or stomach. Other people may receive mental images, words, or thoughts that seem to come out of nowhere. It doesn't matter how it manifests itself, the important thing is to recognize it and give it the importance it deserves. Over time, this practice of paying attention to our intuition will become a habit, and we will begin to notice how it guides us in all areas of our life, from the smallest decisions to the biggest life changes.

Fear and doubt are two of the biggest obstacles to following our intuition. Often, when we feel a strong inclination towards a decision or a path, fear appears to question us: "What if I'm wrong?", "What will others think?", "What if this doesn't work?". It is natural to feel fear when we face the unknown, but it is important not to let this fear drown out the voice of our intuition. Intuition does not push us into dangerous or harmful situations; rather, it guides us toward what is best for us on a deep level. Learning to distinguish between the voice of intuition and the voices of fear or doubt is crucial to using it as a spiritual guide.

Furthermore, intuition does not always take us along the easiest or most comfortable path. Sometimes, it guides us toward decisions that may be difficult or require us to step out of our comfort zone. However, these decisions, although challenging, are often the ones that contribute the most to our spiritual growth and evolution. Intuition is not concerned with what is easy; cares about what is right for our long-term well-being.

The value of intuition as a spiritual guide also manifests itself in our relationships. Intuition can help us understand others on a deeper level, to capture people's emotions and needs beyond the words they say. It helps us connect more authentically and empathetically, allowing us to be more compassionate and understanding. It can also guide us in choosing the people we want to surround ourselves with, attracting those who are aligned with our energy and our values.

Ultimately, following our intuition is an act of trust in ourselves and the universe. It is recognizing that, although we do not always have all the answers, we have a guide within us that is always available to show us the right path. Intuition is an expression of our connection to the divine, to that part of us that always knows what is best for us, even when our conscious mind doesn't. By honoring and following our intuition, we are honoring that connection, allowing our lives to be guided by the wisdom of our soul.

In short, intuition is a powerful spiritual guide that, when listened to and followed, leads us toward a life more aligned with our true essence. Although it can be subtle and sometimes counterintuitive, its value lies in its ability to guide us toward decisions that are in harmony with our well-being and spiritual growth. By learning to listen to and trust our intuition, we are opening the door to a life that is fuller, more authentic, and more connected to who we really are. It is a practice that requires patience, trust and courage, but the results are deeply transformative, leading us to a state of greater peace, wisdom and personal fulfillment.

The Purpose of the Soul

Soul purpose is one of the deepest and most meaningful concepts we can explore in our lives. Since ancient times, human beings have reflected on the reason for their existence, seeking to understand why we are here and what we really come to do in this world. This pursuit is essential to our spiritual well-being, because knowing our soul's purpose not only gives us direction, but also fills us with a sense of meaning and fulfillment that goes beyond the superficial.

Soul purpose can be understood as that special mission or task that each of us has come to fulfill. It is unique to each person, as each soul has a particular set of talents, desires and experiences that differentiate it from others. Finding your soul's purpose is not always obvious or immediate. Many times, it requires a process of self-knowledge, of exploring our passions, our abilities and what makes us feel most alive. We may have to go through various experiences and challenges before we come to a clear understanding of our purpose.

Often, our soul purpose is related to what we love to do most, what we are passionate about and energized by. When we do something that resonates deeply with our soul, we feel a kind of "flow," a sense of being exactly where we need to be, doing what we are supposed to do. This state of flow is an important clue to discovering our purpose. If we pay attention to those moments when we feel most connected and fulfilled, we can begin to identify patterns and themes that guide us toward our purpose.

However, soul purpose is not limited to our passions or talents. It is also about how we can serve others and the world at large. The purpose of each soul is intertwined with the collective well-being. Often, our purpose manifests itself in the way we can make a difference in the lives of others, whether through our work, our relationships, or our everyday actions. This doesn't necessarily mean we have to do something grand or public; Sometimes soul purpose is found in small acts of kindness and compassion that have a profound impact on those around us.

Soul purpose can also change or evolve throughout our lives. As we grow and learn, we may discover new aspects of our purpose, or our mission may expand or adapt to new circumstances. This process of evolution is natural and reflects the fact that the soul's purpose is not something static, but something that develops as we do too. It is important to be open to these changes and be willing to continue exploring and adapting as our purpose reveals itself in new ways.

To find and live our soul's purpose, it is essential that we are in tune with ourselves and our intuition. Meditation, reflection, and time in solitude can help us connect with our essence and listen to the inner voice that guides us toward our purpose. Sometimes the noise of the outside world or the expectations of others can divert our attention from what really matters. Therefore, it is vital to create spaces of silence and reflection where we can listen to what our soul is telling us.

Furthermore, it is essential that we have the courage to follow our purpose, even when it seems difficult or uncertain. Often, the path to fulfilling our purpose is not easy; It can be full of challenges, obstacles and doubts. But it is precisely in these moments of difficulty when our commitment to our purpose is tested and strengthened. By overcoming these challenges, we are not only advancing our path, but we are also developing the inner strength and wisdom that will allow us to fulfill our mission more effectively.

Soul purpose also has a component of personal satisfaction. When we are aligned with our purpose, we experience a sense of fulfillment that cannot be compared to anything else. It is a feeling of being doing exactly what we have come to do, of being in harmony with our true nature. This satisfaction does not depend on external rewards, such as money or recognition, but comes from the deep satisfaction of knowing that we are living according to our deepest truth.

It is important to understand that every purpose is valuable, no matter how big or small it may seem from an external perspective. Sometimes people may underestimate their purpose because it doesn't fit social expectations or because it doesn't seem as impressive as others. However, soul purpose is not measured by its visibility or superficial impact, but by the authenticity and love with which we carry it out. Fulfilling our purpose, no matter how small it may seem, is a valuable contribution to the fabric of life, and has a greater impact than we can imagine.

Finally, it is important to remember that soul purpose is not something that can be forced or rushed. It is a process of discovery that requires patience, openness and trust in divine timing. Sometimes we may feel impatient or frustrated if we don't find our purpose right away, but it is important to remember that each stage of our life is preparing us to fulfill that purpose fully. Every experience, every challenge, every lesson we learn is part of the path toward realizing our spiritual mission.

In short, soul purpose is the deepest reason for our existence, the unique mission that each of us has come to fulfill in this life. Discovering and living this purpose gives us a deep sense of meaning and fulfillment, and allows us to contribute to the well-being of others and the world at large. Although the path to fulfilling our purpose can be challenging, it is also deeply rewarding, leading us to a life of greater authenticity, peace, and personal fulfillment. By listening to our intuition, overcoming challenges, and being in tune with our essence, we can discover and live our soul's purpose in a way that fills us with joy and connects us to the deepest part of our being.

The Power of Gratitude

The power of gratitude is a simple but incredibly transformative concept. Although it may seem like a basic idea, gratitude has the ability to completely change our perspective on life and, as a result, our daily experience. We live in a world that often encourages us to focus on what we don't have, what we are missing, or what is not going well. However, when we decide to focus on what we do have, on what is going well, and on the blessings that already exist in our lives, we begin to see everything from a different perspective, a perspective that is full of light, love and abundance.

Practicing gratitude does not mean ignoring the challenges or difficulties we face. It's not about pretending that everything is perfect when it isn't. Instead, gratitude invites us to recognize and appreciate the good things that exist in our lives, even in the midst of challenges. By focusing on the positive, we are training our minds to see the good in all situations, helping us navigate difficult times with greater resilience and hope. Gratitude connects us to the beauty and abundance of life, reminding us that, despite whatever problems we may be facing, there is always something to be grateful for.

One of the most powerful aspects of gratitude is its ability to change our energetic vibration. When we express gratitude, we are emitting positive, loving energy that attracts more good things to us. It's as if we are sending a message to the universe that says: "I am grateful for what I have, and I am open to receiving more blessings." This positive energy not only affects our external experiences, but also has a profound impact on our inner peace and emotional well-being. We feel calmer, happier, and more at peace when we practice gratitude regularly.

Gratitude also has a positive effect on our relationships. When we express gratitude to the people around us, we strengthen our bonds and create an environment of love and mutual support. Saying "thank you" to someone for something they have done for us, no matter how small, can have a big impact on how that person feels and how we feel ourselves. Gratitude has the power to soften hearts, heal wounds, and build bridges of connection between people. By practicing gratitude in our relationships, we are creating a positive cycle of love and appreciation that benefits everyone involved.

One of the most effective ways to cultivate gratitude is through a daily practice. This can be as simple as taking a few minutes each day to reflect on the things we are grateful for. Some people find it helpful to keep a gratitude journal, where they write down three things they are grateful for each day. This practice forces us to focus on the positive, even on days when things don't seem to be going so well. Over time, this focus on gratitude becomes a habit, and we begin to notice the blessings in our lives more automatically.

Another way to practice gratitude is to express it verbally to others. This can be as simple as saying "thank you" sincerely when someone does something for us, or taking the time to thank the people in our lives for their love, support, and presence. Sometimes a word of gratitude can change a person's day, and we never know the impact our words can have on others. By making gratitude a regular part of our communication, we are spreading positivity and creating an environment of mutual appreciation.

Gratitude also helps us be more present in the moment. When we are grateful, we are recognizing what is happening here and now, rather than worrying about the past or the future. This anchors us in the present and allows us to more fully enjoy life as it is. By practicing gratitude, we learn to see the value of every moment, even the simplest ones, like a delicious meal, a pleasant conversation, or a sunset. These little things, when appreciated with gratitude, become great sources of happiness and satisfaction.

Additionally, gratitude has a positive impact on our physical health. Studies have shown that people who practice gratitude regularly tend to have less stress, less depression, and better sleep patterns. This is because gratitude reduces negative thoughts and worries, which in turn decreases the levels of cortisol, the stress hormone, in our body. By being more relaxed and at peace, our immune system works better, making us less likely to get sick and more able to enjoy good overall health.

It's important to recognize that gratitude is not just something we practice when things are going well. It is an attitude that we can adopt in any circumstance, even in the most difficult moments. In fact, some of the most transformative moments of gratitude can arise during challenges, when we choose to see what we have learned or how we have grown through the difficulty. This type of gratitude, cultivated in the midst of adversity, is deep and powerful, because it helps us find meaning and purpose even in pain.

In short, the power of gratitude is immense and has the ability to transform our lives on many levels. By focusing on what we have, rather than what we lack, we open the door to greater inner peace, happiness and satisfaction. Gratitude improves our relationships, connects us to the present moment, and has tangible benefits for our physical and emotional health. It is a simple but powerful practice that can be incorporated into our daily lives with a little attention and effort. By making gratitude a central part of our existence, we are choosing to see the world through a lens of love and abundance, and in that process, we are creating a life that is filled with joy and purpose.

The Connection with Nature

Connecting with nature is one of the oldest and most profound ways to find peace, balance and well-being. Throughout history, people have turned to nature to find solace, inspiration, and renewal. In modern life, with so many technological distractions and a fast pace of life, we often forget how essential our relationship with the natural world is. However, when we take the time to reconnect with nature, we rediscover an inexhaustible source of wisdom, serenity and healing.

Being in contact with nature offers us a break from the constant stimulation and noise of the urban world. The simple act of walking through a park, sitting by a river, or looking at the stars can have a deeply calming effect on our mind and body. Nature has the ability to return us to a state of simplicity and stillness that is difficult to find elsewhere. In nature, there is no rush, there are no expectations; There is only the present, the sound of the wind in the trees, the murmur of the water and the warmth of the sun on our skin. This simplicity invites us to let go of our worries and be fully present in the moment.

Nature also connects us to something bigger than ourselves. When we find ourselves in a forest or on a mountaintop, it is difficult not to feel a sense of awe and humility at the vastness and beauty of the natural world. This experience can help us put our lives in perspective, reminding us that we are part of a vast, interconnected ecosystem. This sense of connection can be deeply healing, helping us feel less isolated and more connected to the world around us.

In addition to its ability to calm and comfort, nature also has a powerful revitalizing effect. Spending time outdoors, breathing fresh air and moving our body, fills us with energy and vitality. Natural sunlight helps us regulate our circadian rhythms, improving our sleep and mood. Exercising in nature, such as walking, running or swimming, is not only beneficial for our physical health, it also releases endorphins that elevate our mood and make us feel happier and more alive. Nature offers us a way to rejuvenate both physically and mentally, helping us recharge our energies and feel more balanced.

The connection with nature also has a spiritual component. Many find that being in nature helps them feel a deeper connection with the divine, with the sacred. In the stillness of a forest or the vastness of a desert, it is possible to feel the presence of something bigger than ourselves, something that transcends the mundane and connects us with the eternal. This feeling of spiritual connection can be a source of deep peace and comfort, especially in times of uncertainty or pain. Nature, in its infinite beauty and mystery, reminds us that there is something sacred in life itself, something that goes beyond what we can see or understand.

One of the simplest ways to connect with nature is to simply be outdoors, without any agenda or distractions. This means letting go of phones, tasks, and thoughts, and simply allowing ourselves to be present in the natural environment. We can observe the details: the texture of the leaves, the sound of the birds, the smell of the earth after the rain. By doing so, we immerse ourselves in the sensory experience of nature, which helps us disconnect from daily worries and enter a state of calm and mindfulness.

It is also beneficial to learn to recognize and appreciate the rhythms and cycles of nature. Watching how the seasons change, how plants grow, and how animals follow their own natural cycles reminds us that life is a continuous process of change and renewal. By tuning into these cycles, we can find comfort in the idea that everything has its time and place, and that there is a natural order to the universe. This understanding can help us be more patient and accepting of the changes and challenges in our own lives.

Cultivating a relationship with nature does not require great efforts or trips to remote places. We can start in small steps, such as planting a garden, caring for a plant in our home, or simply spending time in a nearby park. These acts allow us to bring nature into our daily lives, reminding us of our connection to the natural world and giving us moments of peace and joy. Even in an urban environment, we can find ways to connect with nature, seeking green spaces, enjoying the sky or feeling the wind on our face.

Finally, it is important to recognize that our connection with nature also implies a responsibility towards it. As we realize how much nature benefits us, we must also be aware of the need to protect and preserve the natural world. This means making conscious decisions to reduce our impact on the environment, supporting sustainable practices and caring for the earth that sustains us. By doing so, we are not only protecting nature for future generations, but we are also strengthening our own spiritual connection with the world around us.

In short, connecting with nature is a vital part of our health and well-being, both physically, emotionally and spiritually. It offers us a haven of peace, a place of renewal and a gateway to a deeper understanding of ourselves and the world around us. By taking the time to be in nature, to observe it, appreciate it and care for it, we are nourishing our soul and reminding ourselves of our innate connection to life in all its forms. In an increasingly accelerated and disconnected world, nature offers us a way back to what is essential, to what is sacred, and to what is true.

Alexa Murphy

The Balance between Soul and Body

The balance between soul and body is essential to live a full and healthy life. In today's society, we often separate the care of the body from the well-being of the soul, but in reality, the two are deeply connected. When we focus on just one of these aspects, we can feel that something is missing, that we are not living in harmony with ourselves. By recognizing the importance of this balance, we can begin to nourish both our body and soul, creating a more integrated and meaningful life.

The body is the vehicle through which we experience life. It is what allows us to move, feel, and interact with the world and with the people around us. Taking care of our body is essential for our physical health, but it also has a direct impact on our emotional and spiritual well-being. When we feel good physically, it is easier to maintain a positive attitude and be in tune with our emotions and our soul. On the other hand, when we neglect our body, we can feel exhausted, unmotivated and disconnected, which affects our ability to fully experience life.

The soul, for its part, is the essence of who we are. It is where our deepest emotions, our beliefs, our desires and our connection to the transcendental reside. Caring for our soul means tending to our emotional and spiritual needs, finding time for introspection, meditation, and connection with the divine, whatever our definition of the divine. When we nourish our soul, we find a sense of purpose, inner peace, and a greater understanding of ourselves and our place in the world.

To achieve true balance between body and soul, it is important to recognize that what affects one also affects the other. For example, when we are stressed or emotionally exhausted, our body may manifest those feelings through illness, fatigue, or pain. Likewise, when we are physically unwell, our emotions and spirit can also be affected, making us feel depressed, anxious or disconnected. That is why it is vital that we approach our well-being in a holistic way, considering both our physical and spiritual needs.

One of the first steps to finding this balance is to pay attention to our body and the signals it sends us. This means being aware of how we feel physically and making adjustments when necessary. If we are tired, we need to rest; if we are tense, we need to relax; If we are sick, we need to take care of ourselves. Taking care of the body is not just about exercise and nutrition, although those are important aspects, but also about listening to our needs and responding to them with compassion and care.

Regular exercise is one of the most effective ways to maintain balance between body and soul. When we move, we not only strengthen our body, but we also release accumulated tension and improve our mood. Exercise can be a form of moving meditation, a time to be present in the here and now, focused on our breathing and the movements of our body. Additionally, regular exercise helps maintain a healthy hormonal balance, which contributes to our emotional and spiritual well-being.

Diet also plays a crucial role in this balance. The foods we eat have a direct impact on how we feel both physically and emotionally. A balanced diet, rich in nutrients, provides us with the energy necessary to function optimally, while processed foods full of sugar can lead us to feel lethargic and unbalanced. By consciously choosing what we eat, we are taking care of our bodies and, at the same time, supporting our emotional and spiritual well-being.

But taking care of the body is not enough if we do not also attend to the needs of the soul. This means taking time for introspection, meditation, prayer, or any other spiritual practice that helps us connect with our deepest selves. These practices allow us to explore our emotions, release what no longer serves us, and find a sense of peace and purpose. By nurturing our soul, we are creating space for our true essence to flourish, which in turn helps us live a more authentic and fulfilling life.

Another important aspect of balance between body and soul is adequate rest. In modern society, we often glorify productivity and always being busy, but this can lead to both physical and emotional exhaustion. Rest is essential for recovery and renewal, allowing us to recharge our energies and maintain a state of balance. Getting enough sleep, taking time to relax, and disconnect from daily demands are vital ways to care for both our body and soul.

It is also useful to consider the environment we live in and how it affects our balance. Our physical environment, such as our home or workplace, can influence how we feel both physically and emotionally. A cluttered or chaotic space can create stress and agitation, while a calm and orderly environment can promote calm and mental clarity. By creating an environment that supports our well-being, we are facilitating balance between body and soul.

Relationships are also a key part of this balance. The connections we have with others can nourish our soul and affect our physical health. Healthy, loving relationships provide us with emotional support, while toxic or conflictual relationships can drain our energies and negatively affect our well-being. It is important to surround ourselves with people who support us, who inspire us and who help us grow, and at the same time, be aware of how our relationships affect our internal balance.

Ultimately, balance between body and soul is an ongoing process, not a final destination. It is something we must cultivate daily, paying attention to our changing needs and making adjustments when necessary. It won't always be perfect, and there will be times when one of these aspects needs more attention than the other. However, by staying aware of the importance of this balance, we can live a more harmonious and fulfilling life.

In short, balance between body and soul is essential for our overall well-being. Taking care of both aspects allows us to live more fully, connected to our essence and in tune with our physical and emotional needs. Through mindful attention to our daily practices, such as exercise, nutrition, rest, and relationships, we can cultivate a balance that supports us in all areas of our lives. By doing so, we not only improve our physical health, but we also enrich our spiritual lives, creating a more meaningful and peaceful existence.

Ancestral Wisdom

Ancestral wisdom is a priceless treasure that has been passed down from generation to generation for thousands of years. This wisdom comes from our ancestors, who lived in harmony with nature, deeply understood the cycles of life, and developed intuitive knowledge about the soul, spirituality, and well-being. Although we live in a modern era full of technological and scientific advances, there is a wealth in ancient teachings that remains relevant today. By exploring this wisdom, we can find answers to many of the questions we face in our lives and discover a path to a more balanced and meaningful existence.

One of the most notable aspects of ancient wisdom is its focus on connection with nature. Our ancestors understood that everything in the universe is interconnected, and that human life is just one part of a much larger ecosystem. This understanding led them to live in tune with the natural rhythms of the earth, respecting the cycles of the seasons, the movement of the stars and the invisible forces that guide life. Instead of seeing nature as something separate from themselves, they viewed it as an extension of their own being. This perspective allowed them to live in harmony with the world around them, taking only what they needed and returning to the land what they could.

Traditional medicine is an example of how ancient wisdom has influenced our understanding of the body and health. Before the advent of modern medicine, cultures around the world developed healing systems based on observation, intuition, and accumulated experience. These traditional medicine systems, such as Ayurveda in India, Traditional Chinese Medicine, and the healing practices of the indigenous peoples of the Americas, are deeply rooted in ancient wisdom. They use herbs, foods, rituals and spiritual practices to balance the body and soul, recognizing that health is the result of a harmonious balance between the two.

In addition to the connection with nature and traditional medicine, ancestral wisdom also offers us teachings about spirituality and the purpose of life. Our ancestors believed that life had a sacred purpose, and that each person had a unique role to play in the fabric of the universe. This sense of purpose was not necessarily linked to material achievements or worldly success, but to the contribution that each individual could make to the well-being of their community and the balance of the natural world. Ancestral spirituality reminds us that we are more than our physical bodies, and that there is a spiritual dimension to life that is equally important to our personal fulfillment.

Ancestral rituals and ceremonies are another expression of this wisdom. Throughout history, cultures around the world have developed rituals to mark important life events, such as birth, puberty, marriage, and death. These rituals not only served to celebrate these moments, but also to connect people with spiritual forces and their ancestors. Through the repetition of these rituals, ancestral wisdom was transmitted from one generation to the next, ensuring that the teachings and values of the community endured over time. These rituals also offered people a way to find meaning and comfort in times of transition and challenge.

Another crucial part of ancient wisdom is the importance of community. In many ancient cultures, the community was the center of social and spiritual life. Decisions were made as a group, and the well-being of each individual was seen as interdependent on the well-being of the community as a whole. This community approach fostered a sense of belonging, mutual support and shared responsibility. In a time where individuality and isolation are common, ancient wisdom reminds us of the importance of cultivating deep and meaningful relationships with others, and of supporting our community in times of need.

Oral transmission was the main means through which ancestral wisdom was preserved and shared. Before the invention of writing, stories, songs, legends, and teachings were passed from one generation to the next through the spoken word. The elders of the community were the guardians of this wisdom, and their role was crucial in keeping the traditions and knowledge alive. Oral transmission not only ensured that the teachings were remembered, but also allowed them to adapt and evolve over time, remaining relevant in a changing world. Today, although we live in a digital world, there is immense value in listening to and learning from the stories of our elders, who still carry with them a rich heritage of ancient wisdom.

Ancestral wisdom is also reflected in traditional arts and crafts. Many cultures developed arts and crafts techniques that were not only functional, but also imbued with spiritual meaning. The creation of objects, such as pottery, textiles, sculptures and paintings, was seen as a sacred act, a way of expressing connection to the spiritual world and honoring ancestors. These objects often contained symbols and patterns that told stories or transmitted spiritual teachings, becoming vehicles of ancient wisdom. By learning and practicing these traditional crafts, we can connect with the creativity and knowledge of our ancestors, and keep alive an essential part of our cultural heritage.

However, it is important to recognize that ancestral wisdom is not something static or immutable. Although it comes from the past, it is alive and continues to evolve. As the world changes, so does our understanding and application of this wisdom. The key is to honor the teachings of our ancestors while adapting them to the realities and challenges of the modern world. This may mean integrating ancient wisdom with new scientific knowledge or combining traditional practices with contemporary approaches. By doing so, we can create a path of life that is both true to our roots and relevant to the present.

In a world that often moves at a frenetic pace and where technology dominates much of our lives, ancient wisdom offers us a reminder of the importance of simplicity, connection and reverence for life. It invites us to slow down, pay attention to the natural rhythms of life, and live in a way that is aligned with our true needs and values. By integrating this wisdom into our lives, we not only honor our ancestors, but we also connect with a deep source of wisdom that can guide us toward a more balanced, fulfilling, and meaningful life.

In conclusion, ancestral wisdom is an invaluable legacy that offers us tools and teachings to live in a more conscious and harmonious way. By learning from the practices, beliefs and knowledge of our ancestors, we can find answers to many of the questions we face today and discover a path to a more balanced and connected life. Although we live in a modern world, there is a wealth of ancient wisdom that remains deeply relevant, and that can help us find peace, purpose and meaning in our lives.

The Mind as a Tool of the Soul

The mind is a powerful tool that allows us to navigate the world, make decisions, solve problems, and create connections with the people and experiences we encounter throughout life. However, beyond these practical functions, the mind also plays a crucial role in our spiritual life, acting as a bridge between the material world and the inner world of the soul. Understanding how the mind can be a tool of the soul is essential to achieving balance and lasting inner peace.

First, it is important to recognize that the mind and soul are not the same, but they are deeply connected. The mind is the part of us that thinks, reasons and processes the information we receive from the outside world. It is where our thoughts, ideas and emotions occur. The soul, on the other hand, is the essence of who we are at our core, beyond temporary thoughts and emotions. It is the eternal, unchanging part of us that connects us to something greater, whether we call it divinity, universal energy, or simply our true nature.

The mind acts as an interpreter of the soul, translating to us the intuitions, desires and deep truths that emerge from our innermost being. Through the mind, the soul can express its desires and guide us towards a life that is aligned with our deepest purpose. However, for the mind to function effectively as a tool of the soul, it needs to be calm and in harmony. When the mind is agitated by stress, fear, or the constant noise of the outside world, it can be difficult to hear the voice of the soul and follow its guidance.

A calm and clear mind is able to tune into the subtle messages of the soul. This mental clarity does not mean that we must eliminate all thoughts or emotions, which would be impossible, but that we must learn to observe them without completely identifying with them. By observing our thoughts and emotions as passing phenomena, we can create an inner space where the soul can manifest and guide our decisions. This process of observation and detachment is essential to using the mind as an effective tool of the soul.

Meditation is one of the most powerful practices to calm the mind and allow the soul to express itself. Through meditation, we train the mind to focus and release unnecessary thoughts that often occupy it. As the mind becomes more serene, a channel of communication opens between the soul and our daily consciousness. In this state, we can receive insights, inspiration, and a deeper understanding of ourselves and the world around us. Meditation not only helps us find inner peace, but also strengthens the connection between mind and soul, allowing us to live more authentically and aligned with our true selves.

Another key aspect to using the mind as a tool of the soul is the power of intention. Our intentions are the seeds that we plant in our minds and that, over time, manifest in our lives. When we align our intentions with the deepest desires of our soul, the mind becomes a vehicle for making those desires come true. This requires a level of self-awareness and clarity about what we really want deep within our being. By setting conscious intentions aligned with our purpose, we can use our mind to create a life that reflects our spiritual values and our desire for inner growth.

However, it is important to be aware that the mind also has its limitations. Although it is a powerful tool, it does not always have all the answers. Sometimes the mind can be trapped by negative thought patterns, doubts and fears that prevent us from hearing the voice of the soul. In these moments, it is helpful to remember that the mind is not the source of our inner truth, but rather an instrument that can be tuned and directed. By practicing self-observation and reflection, we can identify when the mind is acting against the soul's desires and redirect it toward a more harmonious path.

Furthermore, the mind has the ability to create our reality through our perceptions and beliefs. What we believe about ourselves, the world, and our place in it shapes our daily experience. If we have limiting or negative beliefs, our reality can reflect those limits, creating obstacles and challenges that seem difficult to overcome. But when the mind is aligned with the soul, our beliefs become expansive and positive, opening doors and creating opportunities for growth and fulfillment. This ability of the mind to shape our reality is a reminder of the power we have to co-create our lives according to the deepest desires of our soul.

Positive thinking is a tool we can use to align the mind with the soul. Although life is full of challenges and difficult times, maintaining a positive attitude helps us see the opportunities in the midst of difficulties and maintain faith in our spiritual path. It's not about ignoring the negative aspects of life, but about consciously choosing to focus on what lifts us up and brings us closer to our purpose. Positive thinking also strengthens our connection to the soul, allowing us to live with greater hope and confidence in the process of life.

Creativity is another way the mind can serve the soul. When we allow ourselves to be creative, we are expressing the deepest impulses of our soul through the mind. Whether through art, writing, music, or any other form of expression, creativity allows us to shape our ideas, emotions, and inner visions. This creative process is not only a source of joy and satisfaction, but also a way to connect with our deepest essence. By nurturing our creativity, we are using the mind to manifest the beauty and truth that resides in the soul.

Additionally, the mind can be a powerful tool for introspection and self-knowledge. By reflecting on our experiences, thoughts, and emotions, we can gain a deeper understanding of who we are and what we need to grow spiritually. Introspection allows us to explore the deepest parts of our being, discover unconscious patterns, and make conscious changes that bring us closer to our true purpose. Through this process, the mind acts as a mirror that reflects the state of the soul, offering us the opportunity to learn and evolve.

However, for the mind to be an effective tool of the soul, it is essential that we cultivate patience and compassion toward ourselves. The mind can be fickle, sometimes filled with chaotic thoughts and intense emotions. It's easy to get frustrated when we can't fully control our mind or when we find ourselves stuck in negative thought patterns. But by practicing patience and compassion, we can learn to accept the mind as it is, without judging it or trying to force it. This loving approach allows us to work with the mind more effectively, gently guiding it towards a state of greater harmony with the soul.

In short, the mind is a powerful tool that, when used consciously, can serve the soul in its search for peace, purpose and fulfillment. By calming the mind, setting aligned intentions, cultivating positive thinking, and exploring our creativity, we can use the mind to manifest the deepest desires of the soul. Although the mind has its limitations, with patience and compassion we can learn to use it in ways that bring us closer to our true essence and allow us to live a fuller and more meaningful life. The key is to remember that the mind, although powerful, is only an instrument at the service of the soul, and that our true being resides deep within us, beyond the thoughts and emotions that pass through our minds every day. .

The Importance of Spiritual Community

Spiritual community is a fundamental aspect of the journey toward self-knowledge and soul connection. Although the spiritual path is deeply personal and unique to each individual, the company of others who share a similar approach can be invaluable. The importance of a spiritual community lies in the strength that is generated by uniting people with a common purpose: inner growth, mutual support, and the search for greater spiritual understanding. This union not only offers us a sense of belonging, but also provides us with the tools and encouragement necessary to face the challenges of the spiritual path.

One of the main benefits of belonging to a spiritual community is the support you receive. The spiritual path can often be lonely and challenging, filled with questions and moments of uncertainty. In those moments, having a network of people who understand and share our concerns can make a big difference. In a spiritual community, we find people willing to listen to us, share their own experiences, and offer perspectives we might not have considered.

This mutual support helps us feel less alone and more capable of facing the difficulties that will inevitably come our way.

In addition to emotional support, spiritual community gives us the opportunity to learn from others. Each person in the community brings with them their own set of unique experiences, knowledge, and perspectives. By sharing these stories and teachings, everyone in the community is enriched. Spiritual practices, books read, meditations performed, and reflections shared become a source of continuous learning for all members. This sharing of wisdom helps us expand our understanding and grow spiritually, learning not only from our own experiences, but also from those of others.

Another important aspect of spiritual community is the motivation that comes from connection with others. Sometimes on our spiritual path, we can lose motivation or feel stuck. It is in these moments that the community can act as a catalyst for our progress. Seeing others move forward, face their own challenges, and maintain their dedication to spiritual practice can inspire us to keep going, even when things get difficult. The collective energy of a spiritual community can lift our spirits and remind us why we began this journey in the first place.

Spiritual community also plays a crucial role in creating a safe space for exploration and growth. In a truly spiritual community, openness, authenticity, and respect are valued. This environment allows members to be themselves, without fear of being judged or misunderstood. Being able to express our doubts, fears and discoveries in a space where we know we will be heard and supported is essential for spiritual growth. This environment of acceptance allows us to be vulnerable and explore the deepest parts of our being, knowing that we are surrounded by people who understand and support us.

Additionally, spiritual community helps keep us accountable on our spiritual path. It's easy to let go of our spiritual practices or lose sight of our goals when we're alone. However, in a community, there is a sense of mutual commitment that encourages us to move forward. By participating in group activities, such as meditations, studies, or rituals, we commit not only to our own practice, but also to the community as a whole. This collective commitment helps us maintain discipline and consistency in our path, knowing that our growth not only benefits ourselves, but also the community as a whole.

The spiritual community is also a place where achievements and personal growth can be celebrated. On the spiritual path, we often experience moments of breakthrough, understanding, or healing that are meaningful to us. Sharing these moments with others who understand their importance amplifies the joy and sense of accomplishment. Celebrations within the community, whether rituals, ceremonies or simply gatherings to share experiences, create a sense of unity and strengthen ties between members. These moments of celebration remind us that we are not alone on our journey and that our personal achievements are also a source of joy for the entire community.

Another valuable aspect of spiritual community is the diversity of perspectives it offers. Although members of the community may share a common approach to spirituality, each person has their own way of understanding and living that spirituality. This diversity is a source of enrichment for all members, as it opens up new ways of thinking and seeing the world. By listening to the experiences and beliefs of others, we can expand our own understanding and find new ways to connect with our soul. This diversity also teaches us the importance of tolerance, respect and acceptance of differences, values that are essential on any spiritual path.

It is important to mention that the spiritual community does not necessarily have to be a large congregation or a formal group. Sometimes a spiritual community can be as small as a couple of friends who support each other on their spiritual path. What really matters is not the size of the community, but the quality of the relationships and the sense of connection that is created. What is essential is that there is a space where people can come together to share, learn and grow together in their spirituality.

Additionally, spiritual community can have a positive impact on society at large. As members of a spiritual community grow and transform, they often carry with them a desire to contribute to the well-being of others. This desire can manifest itself in concrete actions, such as volunteering, participating in community projects, or simply the act of bringing compassion and understanding to daily relationships. In this way, the spiritual community not only benefits its members, but also has the potential to positively radiate into the outside world, promoting values of love, peace and unity.

Ultimately, spiritual community offers us a constant reminder that although our spiritual path is unique, we are not alone in our quest. The company of others who share our values and vision strengthens us and encourages us to keep going, even in the most difficult times. By coming together in community, we create a space where we can grow, learn and celebrate together, supporting each other on our journey toward greater connection with our soul. This connection with others is, in itself, an expression of spirituality, as it reminds us that we are all interconnected and that our spiritual lives are enriched when we share our experience with others.

The importance of spiritual community cannot be underestimated. It is a fundamental pillar on our path towards self-knowledge and connection with the soul. Through community, we find support, learning, motivation and a sense of belonging that help us stay strong on our path. It offers us a safe space where we can be ourselves and explore the depths of our spirituality. And, above all, it reminds us that, although the spiritual journey is personal, it does not have to be lonely. As we share our journey with others, we discover that spirituality is both an individual experience and a collective experience, and that in that union we find a strength and wisdom that helps us achieve a fuller and more meaningful life.

Overcoming Spiritual Challenges

Overcoming spiritual challenges is a fundamental aspect of the journey towards self-knowledge and connection with our deepest essence. These challenges can arise at any time and, although they are often difficult to face, they are valuable opportunities to grow and strengthen our spirit. As we progress on our spiritual path, it is inevitable that we will encounter obstacles that will cause us to question our beliefs, our decisions, and in some cases, even our ability to continue. However, it is precisely in these times of difficulty that we have the opportunity to learn important lessons and develop greater spiritual resilience.

One of the most common challenges we face on our spiritual path is doubt. Doubt can manifest itself in many ways: doubts about our beliefs, about the purpose of our spiritual quest, or even about our ability to move forward on this path. At times, doubt can seem overwhelming, especially when we face difficult situations or when we feel disconnected from our spirituality. However, it is important to remember that doubt is not something negative in itself. In fact, it can be a powerful tool for spiritual growth. When we face doubt, we are presented with the opportunity to dig deeper into our beliefs, ask deeper questions, and seek answers that truly resonate with our soul. Doubt invites us to explore and find a more authentic and solid understanding of our spirituality.

Another significant spiritual challenge is fear. Fear can arise from many sources: fear of change, fear of the unknown, fear of losing what is familiar or comfortable. On the spiritual path, we are often faced with the need to let go of old beliefs, thought patterns, or behaviors that no longer serve us. This process can be terrifying, as it involves stepping into the unknown and being willing to give up what we know. However, it is precisely by facing and overcoming these fears that we can truly experience profound growth. Fear teaches us to trust ourselves and the spiritual process, to find the courage to move forward, even when we cannot see clearly what awaits us. Overcoming fear allows us to open ourselves to new experiences and a deeper understanding of ourselves and the world around us.

Suffering is another of the great spiritual challenges. Throughout life, we all experience moments of pain, whether physical, emotional or spiritual. These times can be extremely difficult to endure and often lead us to question our faith or feel disconnected from our spirituality. However, suffering can also be a powerful catalyst for spiritual growth. Through suffering, we can learn important lessons about compassion, resilience, and inner strength. It offers us the opportunity to deepen our understanding of life and develop greater empathy towards others. Although it is natural to want to avoid suffering, it is important to remember that it is an inevitable part of the human experience and that, by facing it with courage and acceptance, we can transform it into a source of growth and wisdom.

Loneliness is another challenge that many people face on their spiritual path. At certain times in our lives, we can feel disconnected from others or even from ourselves. This sense of loneliness can be especially acute on the spiritual path, where we often face questions and challenges that are not always understood or shared by those around us. However, solitude can also be an opportunity to deepen our connection with our inner being and with the divine. In the stillness of solitude, we can find space for reflection, meditation and contemplation, allowing us to hear the voice of our soul and strengthen our connection to our spirituality. By learning to be comfortable in our own company, we develop greater confidence in ourselves and our ability to find answers and guidance within ourselves.

Another spiritual challenge is attachment. We often cling to things, people, or ideas that provide us with a sense of security or identity. However, attachment can become an obstacle on our spiritual path, as it prevents us from moving forward and keeps us stuck in the past. Learning to let go of attachment does not mean giving up what is important to us, but rather learning to relate to it in a more balanced and detached way. This allows us to free up the space necessary for new experiences and opportunities to come into our lives. By letting go of attachment, we learn to trust the flow of life and accept changes with greater serenity and equanimity.

Demotivation is another obstacle that can arise on the spiritual path. Sometimes, after having started with a lot of enthusiasm and dedication, we may find ourselves at a point where we lose interest or energy to continue. This can happen for a variety of reasons: perhaps we are not seeing the results we expected, or perhaps we are feeling overwhelmed by the challenges we have faced. At these times, it is important to remember that the spiritual path is not always linear and that it is natural to have ups and downs. Demotivation invites us to reflect on our expectations and readjust our approach. Maybe we need to change our spiritual practice, try something new, or simply give ourselves some time to rest and recharge. By recognizing and accepting these moments of demotivation, we can find ways to rekindle our passion for the spiritual path and continue moving forward with renewed vigor.

The temptation to abandon the spiritual path is perhaps one of the most difficult challenges to overcome. In times of crisis or difficulty, it may seem easier to give up our spiritual practices or our ideals. However, it is precisely in these moments when we most need to hold on to our spirituality. Getting off the road may provide temporary relief, but in the long term, it can lead us to feel even more lost and disconnected. Instead of giving up, it is important to remember why we started this journey in the first place and what values and principles really matter in our lives. By finding the strength to persevere, even in the darkest moments, we develop greater resilience and a deeper connection to our soul.

It is crucial to remember that spiritual challenges are not signs that we are failing on our path, but rather opportunities to deepen and strengthen our spirituality. Each challenge offers us the chance to learn something new about ourselves, about the world, and about our relationship with the divine. By facing these challenges with courage, patience, and an open mind, we can transform difficulties into valuable lessons and move forward with greater clarity and purpose on our spiritual journey.

Furthermore, it is important to recognize that we are not alone in overcoming these challenges. Whether through connecting with a spiritual community, the support of a mentor or spiritual guide, or simply through seeking resources and practices to help us grow stronger, there are always ways to find the support we need to overcome challenges. obstacles in our path. By seeking and accepting help when we need it, we allow ourselves to move forward with greater confidence and determination.

In short, spiritual challenges are an inevitable and essential part of the path to inner growth and connection with our soul. Although they may be difficult to face, they are also opportunities to learn, grow, and strengthen our spirituality. By approaching these challenges with an attitude of openness and acceptance, we can transform them into catalysts for our spiritual development and find a deeper sense of purpose and peace in our lives.

The Continuous Evolution of the Soul

The continuous evolution of the soul is a concept that invites us to understand that our spiritual growth is not a process that has an end point, but rather it is an endless journey. From the moment we are born, our souls are in a constant state of development, learning and transformation. This growth does not stop at any time in our lives; On the contrary, every experience, every challenge, and every achievement are steps on the path to a deeper understanding of ourselves and our connection to the universe.

The idea of the continuous evolution of the soul suggests that our existence is a dynamic and constantly changing process. We are not the same today as we were yesterday, and we will not be the same tomorrow. With each new day, we gain new perspectives, learn new lessons, and face new opportunities to grow. This growth may be subtle and gradual, or it may be more pronounced, as a result of significant experiences or moments of profound change. The important thing is to recognize that, regardless of the speed or the way in which it occurs, the evolution of our soul is a natural and inevitable process.

On this path of evolution, it is essential to understand that there is no final "goal" that we must achieve. Often in life, we set goals and work toward them, thinking that once we achieve them, we are done. However, when it comes to spiritual growth, there is no final destination. There is always more to learn, more to discover and more to experience. This perspective can be liberating, allowing us to enjoy the journey instead of obsessing about getting to a specific point. It invites us to live in the present, to appreciate each moment and accept that each stage of our life has something valuable to offer.

One of the most beautiful aspects of the continued evolution of the soul is that each person follows their own unique path. There are no two souls that evolve in the same way. What is meaningful to one person may not be meaningful to another, and that's okay. Each of us has our own story, our own challenges and our own lessons to learn.

Comparing ourselves to others in terms of spiritual growth is unhelpful and can be counterproductive. Instead of focusing on how we are doing in relation to others, it is more beneficial to focus our attention on our own progress and how we can continue to move forward on our personal path.

Soul evolution also involves a certain willingness to change and adapt. Throughout our lives, we face situations that challenge us to reconsider our beliefs, adopt new ways of thinking, and let go of old patterns that no longer serve us. This process of change may be uncomfortable or even painful, but it is essential for our spiritual growth. By being open to change, we allow our soul to continue evolving and adapting to the new realities we face. It is in this constant flow and adaptation that we truly find the meaning and purpose of our lives.

Another crucial aspect of the soul's continued evolution is lifelong learning. Every experience, whether positive or negative, offers us an opportunity to learn something new. Sometimes the lessons we learn are obvious and easy to understand, but other times, they may be more subtle and require deeper reflection. It is important to be attentive and aware of these lessons, since they are what guide us on our spiritual path. Even in the most difficult times, when it seems like there is nothing good that can come out of a situation, there is a lesson waiting to be discovered. By adopting an attitude of continuous learning, we can transform each experience into an opportunity to grow and evolve.

The evolution of the soul is also influenced by our relationships with others. Through our interactions with friends, family, coworkers, and strangers, we have the opportunity to learn and grow. Every relationship we have teaches us something about ourselves, whether it's patience, compassion, empathy or forgiveness. Through our relationships, we can see our own strengths and weaknesses reflected, allowing us to work on those areas of our lives that need more attention. By cultivating healthy, meaningful relationships, we support the evolution of our soul and contribute to the well-being of those around us.

In the context of the continued evolution of the soul, it is also important to recognize the importance of self-reflection and introspection. Taking time to reflect on our actions, thoughts, and emotions allows us to gain a deeper understanding of who we are and where we are headed. Introspection helps us identify areas in which we need to grow and develop a greater awareness of our motivations and desires. As we know ourselves better, we can make decisions more aligned with our true selves, allowing us to evolve more consciously and deliberately.

It is essential to understand that the evolution of the soul is not always linear. There will be times when we will feel like we are making great strides, and others when it will feel like we are stagnating or even going backwards. These ups and downs are a natural part of the spiritual growth process. Sometimes periods of apparent stagnation are actually moments of integration and assimilation of the lessons we have learned. It is during these times that our inner being is processing and preparing the ground for a new level of evolution. By accepting these cycles and trusting the process, we can find peace and contentment in our spiritual path, no matter what stage we are at.

Finally, the continued evolution of the soul reminds us that we are not alone on this journey. Although each person follows their own path, we are all connected on a deeper level. As we evolve individually, we also contribute to the collective evolution of humanity. Our actions, thoughts and decisions have an impact on the world around us, and by striving to grow and evolve in positive ways, we also help raise the collective consciousness. This sense of connection and shared responsibility motivates us to continue forward on our spiritual path, knowing that our growth not only benefits our soul, but also the entire human being.

In short, the continued evolution of the soul is a never-ending process of growth, learning, and transformation. There is no final destination, but rather a constant journey toward a deeper understanding of ourselves and our connection to the universe. Through openness to change, lifelong learning, meaningful relationships, and self-reflection, we can advance our spiritual path and contribute to collective well-being. By embracing this process of continuous evolution, we find deeper purpose and meaning in our lives, and come closer to our true essence.

www.ingramcontent.com/pod-product-compliance
Lightning Source LLC
Chambersburg PA
CBHW022135150726
47992CB00002B/604